RUBY-THROATED HUMMINGBIRDS

James E. Gerholdt
ABDO & Daughters

Published by Abdo & Daughters, 4940 Viking Drive, Suite 622, Edina, Minnesota 55435.

Copyright © 1997 by Abdo Consulting Group, Inc., Pentagon Tower, P.O. Box 36036, Minneapolis, Minnesota 55435 USA. International copyrights reserved in all countries. No part of this book may be reproduced in any form without written permission from the publisher.

Printed in the United States.

Cover and Interior Photo credits: Peter Arnold, Inc.

Edited by Julie Berg

Library of Congress Cataloging-in-Publication Data

Gerholdt, James E., 1943—
        Ruby-throated hummingbirds/James E. Gerholdt.
              p.   cm. -- (birds)
        Includes index.
        Summary: Describes the physical characteristics, habitat, and habits of one of the smallest of all birds.
        ISBN 1-56239-586-6
        1. Ruby-throated hummingbird--Juvenile literature. [1. hummingbirds.] I. Title. II. Series: Gerholdt, James E., 1943—Birds.
        QL696.A558G47   1996
        598.8'99--dc20   95-48185
                                                      CIP
                                                     AC

Contents

RUBY-THROATED HUMMINGBIRDS

Ruby-throated hummingbirds belong to one of the 28 **orders** of **birds**. They are in the same order as swifts and whip-poor-wills. They are called hummingbirds because of the humming sound they make when they fly and **hover**.

Birds are **vertebrates**. This means they have backbones, just like humans. Birds are also **warm-blooded**.

Ruby-throated hummingbirds are one of the most common hummingbirds. You may have seen one in your own garden. Their wings flutter so fast, you can't see them move! Sometimes people mistake these birds for large moths.

Hummingbirds make a
humming sound when
they fly.

SIZES

Ruby-throated hummingbirds are one of the smallest kinds of hummingbirds. And hummingbirds are the smallest of all **birds**.

The females are a little larger than the males, and weigh .1 to .16 ounces (2.8 to 5.4 g). The males weigh .08 to .13 ounces (2.4 to 3.6 g). From the tip of the **bill** to the tip of the tail, they are only 3 to 3 3/4 inches (7.6 to 9.5 cm). The **wingspan** is 4 to 4 3/4 inches (10.1 to 12.1 cm).

Opposite page: The ruby-throated hummingbird is very small and has red feathers around its throat.

SHAPES

Ruby-throated hummingbirds have slender bodies. Their wings are long and pointed, and sweep back from the body—like the wings of a jetplane.

The wing muscles are very strong, and can beat at speeds of up to 75 strokes a second. Because of this, they have been timed at speeds of 50 to 60 miles per hour (80 to 96.5 kilometers per hour). They can also **hover**, just like a helicopter!

The **bill** is long and straight like a needle. This makes it possible for them to feed deep inside of flowers. The males' tails are forked, the females' are rounded. Their legs are short and their feet are small.

Opposite page: Ruby-throated hummingbirds have long, pointed wings and thin bodies.

COLORS

The sight of a male ruby-throated hummingbird is something to remember! It is one of the jewels of the **bird** world. The throat is a bright fire-red. The back is a metallic green. The chest is gray.

The female ruby-throated hummingbird also has a metallic green back, but her throat is white. She also has white spots on her tail.

A female ruby-throated hummingbird.

A male ruby-throated hummingbird.

WHERE THEY LIVE

The ruby-throated hummingbird is found all over the eastern United States and southern Canada, and as far west as Alberta. It also has been seen in Alaska, Cuba, Bermuda, Ontario, and Labrador.

During the winter the ruby-throated hummingbird **migrates** to Mexico and Central America—a distance of 500 miles (805 km) or more!

The ruby-throated hummingbird is found where there are flowers. It is attracted to those that are red. Gardens and the edges of woods are good places to look for these **birds**.

The ruby-throated hummingbird is attracted to flowers.

SENSES

Ruby-throated hummingbirds have the same five senses as humans. Their sense of taste is most important. It helps them find the sweet and sugary **nectar** they need to **survive**.

Ruby-throated hummingbirds have good eyesight. They can see colors and are especially attracted to red.

Their senses also help them **migrate** across the Gulf of Mexico without losing their way. Unlike many other birds, they migrate during the daylight hours.

Opposite page: A ruby-throated hummingbird feeding on a rhododendron.

DEFENSE

Because they are so small, ruby-throated hummingbirds have **enemies** that larger **birds** don't.

Sometimes they are caught in webs, and become dinner for spiders. Dragonflies and praying mantis are insect enemies. Frogs may also jump out of the water and grab these birds.

But one of the most dangerous enemies to ruby-throated hummingbirds are glass windows. If they fly into one, they can die!

Opposite page: A hummingbird nestled safely in its nest.

FOOD

Nectar is the ruby-throated hummingbird's most important food. They get nectar from flowers.

Their ability to **hover** allows them to stick their long **bills** deep into flowers. Their long tongues are shaped like a tube with a brush at the end. This is what they use to remove the nectar.

Ruby-throated hummingbirds also eat insects and spiders, both of which are found on the flowers they feed on. Hummingbirds often pick spiders from their webs and eat them.

Opposite page: The ruby-throated hummingbird gets nectar from the flower.

BABIES

All ruby-throated hummingbirds hatch from eggs. The eggs are tiny, and only measure .3 by .5 inches (8 x 13 mm). They are white with a smooth shell, and there are usually two laid at a time.

The nest is built in trees, usually 10 to 20 feet (3 to 6 m) above the ground. It measures 1 to 1 3/4 inches (25 to 44 mm) across and is 3/4 of an inch (19 mm) deep.

The eggs take about two weeks to hatch. The babies leave the nest when they are around 19 days old.

Opposite page: A female hummingbird with her babies in their nest.

GLOSSARY

bill - A bird's beak

bird (BURD) - A feathered animal with a backbone whose front limbs are wings.

enemy - Something dangerous or harmful to something else.

feather (FETH-urr) - The light, flat structures covering a bird's body.

hover - To remain suspended in the air.

migration (mi-GRASH-un) - The moving from one area to another.

nectar (NECK-turr) - A sweet liquid that comes from flowers.

order (OAR-der) - A grouping of animals.

survive (ser-VIVE)- To live longer than.

vertebrate (ver-ta-BRAIT) - An animal with a backbone.

warm-blooded (warm-BLUD-ed) - Regulating body temperature at a constant level, from inside the body.

wingspan (WING-spann) - The distance from the tip of one wing to the other.

INDEX